D1402805

WHAT IT MEANS TO BE
SERIES

PUBLISHER	Joseph R. DeVarennes
PUBLICATION DIRECTOR	Kenneth H. Pearson
ADVISORS	Roger Aubin
	Robert Furlonger
EDITORIAL MANAGER	Jocelyn Smyth
EDITORS	Ann Martin
	Shelley McGuinness
	Robin Rivers
	Mayta Tannenbaum
ARTISTS	Summer Morse
	Barbara Pileggi
	Steve Pileggi
	Mike Stearns
PRODUCTION MANAGER	Ernest Homewood
PRODUCTION ASSISTANTS	Catherine Gordon
	Kathy Kishimoto
PUBLICATION ADMINISTRATOR	Anna Good

Canadian Cataloguing in Publication Data

Langdon, Anne
    What it means to be—a leader

(What it means to be; 18)
ISBN 0-7172-2234-9

1. Leadership — Moral and ethical aspects — Juvenile literature.
I. Pileggi, Steve.   II. Title.   III. Title: A leader.   IV. Series.

BF637.L4L36 1987   j177   C87-095060-6

WHAT IT MEANS TO BE...

A LEADER

Written by
Anne Langdon

Illustrated by
Steve Pileggi

When a situation needs changing, a leader will do something about it.

Tammy and her father were walking by the pond in the park one day when she noticed the ducks, geese and swans building their nests. The ducks and geese were well out of the way, but the swans were nesting in the reeds very close to the footpath.

"The swans are very busy," said Tammy.

"They sure are," answered her father.

Tammy frowned. "Dad, look at those dogs. They're chasing that swan off her nest. What can we do?"

"It's okay. The dogs' owner is leashing them. All dogs have to be on leashes here."

"But, Dad," Tammy cried. "Now those people are getting too close. The swans will get scared. We have to do something."

"What do you suggest?" asked her dad.

"Let's go tell them at the park office tomorrow when it opens."

Don't wait for other people to solve problems. When you see something that needs doing, be willing to take the first step toward getting it done.

A good leader always makes sure that a project is completed.

Early the next morning Tammy and her father set out for the park.

"Where are you going so early?" asked Mitchell.

"I'm going to save the swans," she said.

"Sounds important. Can I come too?" he asked.

"We're glad to have you along," said her dad.

At the park office, Tammy explained the problem and suggested they put up a fence to protect the swans. The wardens listened to her and thanked her for bringing the problem to their attention.

Two days later Tammy and Mitchell were at the pond again. No fences had been put up.

Tammy was upset. "I think we should go back to the office. Maybe they forgot my idea." The wardens in the office were pleased to see them.

"Don't worry, Tammy, we've ordered wire fences to protect the swans and their nests. They should be up by tomorrow. And, thanks again."

A good plan for solving a problem is not enough. Good leaders know they must follow through to make sure the plan is carried out.

A leader works toward a goal.

Janice and Jason's mother was very excited. She was looking forward to starting her new job after the weekend.

"It's something I've always wanted to do," she said to the family at the dinner table. "And now I'm getting my chance."

Janice was happy for her mother and wanted to help her celebrate—but what could she do? "I know!" she whispered to Jason as they were getting ready for bed. "Let's give Mom a surprise party!"

"All right!" Jason answered.

"We'll have to ask Dad if it's okay," Janice added.

"I think that's a wonderful idea," her father said. "And I'll do whatever I can to help you."

"Let's have a surprise dinner with Mom's favorite food and a cake," suggested Janice.

"Yeah!" chorused her dad and brother.

When Janice told Hannah about the big plan, Hannah said, "It will never work. You're wasting your time. Kids don't give parties for parents, it's the other way around."

"Not this time," Janice said. "This time it's a special party just for my mom. Dad's helping."

"See, that's what I mean!" cried Hannah. "Kids can't do stuff like that."

"Yes, I can!" Janice cried. "It was my idea and it will be the best party ever with balloons and cake and a special song for Mom about her new job."

After thinking for a while, Hannah said, "It does sound like fun. I bet your mom will be really surprised."

The day of the party, Janice got up earlier than usual. All through breakfast she looked at her brother across the table and giggled. Trying not to laugh made them laugh even harder.

"What are you up to?" their mother asked.

"Oh, nothing," they answered, each trying to keep a straight face.

It was Jason's job to keep their mother busy while Janice and their father decorated the house. "Don't forget to pick me up after school," Jason said.

"And don't worry about fixing dinner," their father added. "I'll make something simple."

Later that day, while Jason was out with their mother doing errands, Janice and their father were busy decorating the dining room, setting the table, wrapping the present and trying to cook dinner. It was the most fun they'd had in a long time.

When Jason came in with his mother, he ran over to his father and sister. Together they yelled, "Congratulations on your new job!"

It was the first time Janice and Jason had ever seen someone laugh and cry at the same time.

"Who thought of this?" their mother asked.

"It was Janice's idea," said Jason.

"But I got a lot of help from Dad and Jason," Janice added.

If you plan carefully and work toward a goal, you will be pleased with the results of your efforts.

Being a leader means believing in yourself.

Dylan and Bobby were walking home from school. Eva was ahead of them on the sidewalk, too far away to talk to. Before they had a chance to catch up to her, she turned up her driveway and went indoors.

When Dylan got home he wondered what Eva's house was like inside. He had never been to her house or asked her to play at his house. There was a lot he didn't know about her. "Maybe I could ask her to my place after school someday."

That night before bed, Dylan asked his father what he thought of the plan.

"I think it's a great idea."

"But what if she doesn't want to play with me?" Dylan asked, suddenly feeling nervous.

"How will you ever know if you don't ask her?" his father said with a laugh.

As Dylan was waiting to go into school the next morning, he saw Eva. "Would you like to come to my house after school sometime?" he asked.

"To your house?" Eva asked. "When?"

"Whenever you like," Dylan replied.

"Oh, yes!" she cried. "That would be fun." After thinking for a moment, she added, "I will tell my mother and she will want to make a cake. It's okay to bring a cake?"

Dylan laughed out loud. "Of course it's okay." Then with a smile he added, "Maybe you can come over to my place *every* day after school."

If you want to accomplish something, you have to believe in yourself and your ideas.

Good leaders don't give up after running into difficulties.

Mitchell was visiting Tammy one Saturday afternoon. They didn't know if they felt like staying inside or going outdoors. They were a little bored.

"I feel hungry," sighed Tammy.

"Me too," Mitchell said.

"Let's ask my dad if we can make popcorn," Tammy suggested.

"Too bad we don't have a movie to go with it."

Just then, Tammy's eyes lit up. She was getting an idea. "Why don't we make a whole bunch and sell it? Maybe that way we can make enough to go see a real movie!"

Her father agreed and helped them make a big bowl. "Popcorn is a good snack to sell," he said. "It doesn't cost very much, it's easy for grownups to help you make and it's good for you."

Mitchell and Tammy ran outside and waited for a customer. Colette helped by making a big, bright sign. It said: Popcorn for Sale. Low, Low Prices.

Soon Kim wandered over with Lee. "I'll take an extra large bag," she said, "so I'll have enough to share with Lee."

"One extra large bag coming up!" said Tammy.

Paul asked for a regular bag. While everyone was busy, Lee reached over and grabbed the edge of the big popcorn bowl. He gave it a yank. All the popcorn spilled, and the big plastic bowl landed on his head.

At first, Tammy was angry that Lee had ruined her plans. Then she couldn't help laughing when she saw how surprised and funny he looked with the bowl on his head.

"I'll ask Dad to make some more."

"And I'll help clean up," Mitchell offered.

"What are *you* going to do, Lee?" Paul asked. Lee answered by lifting the bowl off his head and holding it out.

"He's all ready to be your first customer," laughed Kim.

If you think hard and keep your sense of humor, you can often come up with a way to carry on when something has disrupted your plans.

Being a leader means being prepared for changes in plans.

All the kids were back at school and Ryan began to miss summertime activities. It was early in September and the weather was still warm.

After supper one evening, when his friends were wandering around, Ryan put forward his idea.

"Why don't we have a picnic at the beach this weekend? Everyone can bring one thing to share and there will be lots to eat."

All the kids thought this was a great idea. Ryan had made a list of the different things they would need, and everyone took turns asking him how they could contribute.

Suddenly Bobby said, "What if it rains?"

"Let's just hope it doesn't," Ryan answered. "But if it does, my parents said we could have the picnic in my recreation room instead."

"Yeahhhhhhh!" all the kids cried.

Planning special events and looking forward to them can be a lot of fun. It is always a good idea to make alternative arrangements in case things don't work out as you expected.

Leaders know it is a mistake to be too bossy.

Paul and Dylan looked out the window and wondered if the rain would ever stop. Dylan was at Paul's house watching a dance show on TV.

"Those guys move pretty fast," Dylan said. "But I bet we could do that too."

"Sure," Paul replied. "It just takes practice. See—watch this dance I made up."

"That's wild!" cried Dylan, jumping up. "Now look at this."

Soon the boys were leaping and dancing and flinging themselves all over the room.

"What are you kids up to?" Paul's father asked from the living room.

"We're having a dance contest," Paul cried.

"Maybe you'd better do it someplace else. You're making an awful racket."

"We could do in the garage," Paul suggested.

"And I could get my cassette player and tapes I got for Christmas," Dylan said.

Soon, they were dancing and laughing in the garage. Kim and Colette heard them as they were walking to the library.

"What are you guys doing?" Colette asked.

"We're having a dance contest," Paul answered.

"Can we join too?" Kim asked.

"Yeah, sure," Paul replied. "It's okay if we make a racket out here."

"I'll go get some of my tapes," Colette said.

"Just a minute!" Paul objected crossly. "It's my dance contest and I'm choosing the music."

Kim and Colette were suddenly silent and looked down at the ground. Dylan was quiet too. Then Dylan said to Paul, "Everybody should have a turn."

"Yeah," Kim agreed.

"If we can't take turns, I don't want to play," Colette said finally.

Just then Paul realized that it's pretty hard to have a dance contest if no one wants to be in it.

"Okay, go get your tapes," he said. "While we're waiting, Dylan and I can think of a prize and work on the contest rules."

Forcing people to do what you want doesn't make you a leader. Leaders encourage others to share in the work and planning of their projects.

Good leaders listen to other people's views.

Bobby's aunt gave him a large red ball for his birthday. It was his favorite ball to throw against the side of the garage.

He took it out with him after breakfast hoping someone might come by to play. There were all sorts of games he could play alone, but he was in the mood for company.

"What are you doing?" Kim called from across the street.

"Just playing catch," Bobby answered.

"Why don't we play a game?" Kim said once she had crossed the street.

"Sure, but we'll need more people," he pointed out.

"We can go down to the playground," suggested Kim. "I'm sure we'll find some kids there."

"Let's play dodge ball," Bobby suggested to his friends in the playground. They all thought that was a good idea, but they couldn't decide on the rules.

"If the ball hits you, your whole team goes out," stated Paul.

"Not the team, just one person," Kim said.

"And I think we should only hit below the knees," Colette said.

"No way!" Paul shouted. "That's no fun."

"Yes it is!" Colette cried.

"It is not!" Paul yelled.

Bobby wanted friends to play with, but he didn't want to be in the middle of any arguments. "Listen," Bobby suggested. "Why don't we play with the same rules as last time for one game and then Paul's way for another game?" That seemed fair, and all the kids agreed.

"But which team goes first?" Colette asked.

"I'll think of a number, write it down and the rest of you guess. Whoever comes closest, their team will go first," he said.

Soon they were all playing happily together.

Listening to other people's ideas and treating everyone fairly helps a leader avoid arguments when working or playing in a group.

Leaders are always prepared to learn from others.

Hannah, Kim and Tammy were lying on their backs in the park, looking at the orange autumn leaves.

"Let's ride our bikes," Kim suggested.

"But it's no fun for us," Hannah said with a sigh. "We don't have a mountain bike like you."

Kim jumped up. "I'll let you borrow mine."

Once Kim had pulled her bike from the garage, Hannah got on it. Tammy leaned over and squeezed the front tire. "You should put in more air."

"But you've never ridden a mountain bike before," Kim said, "so how would you know?"

Kim's father came over and felt the tire. "Tammy is right," he said. "I'll get out the pump."

At first Kim felt cross that she had been wrong. Her father said, "It's a good thing Tammy pointed that out. It's not good to ride a bike when the tires are too soft."

"Thanks, Tammy," Kim smiled. "I learned something from you and now you can learn something from me."

No matter how much you know, you can always learn from others.

Not everyone can be a leader.

Hannah was on her way to the playground to meet her friends. It was a beautiful autumn day—warm and sunny. "There won't be too many more days like this before it starts to get cold and winter comes," she thought. "Maybe we should plan one last picnic in the park."

At the playground Hannah saw Colette, Bobby, Dylan and Janice. "Hey, everybody!" she shouted. "I have a great idea. Let's have a picnic with races and games and food and prizes and—"

"Slow down, Hannah," said Bobby. "What kind of races?"

"Um-m-m, I'm not sure," sighed Hannah.

"What kind of food do you want? What should I bring?" asked Colette.

"Well . . . um-m-m . . ."

"Hannah, you don't have any answers," sneered Dylan. "I say let's forget it." The kids ran off after Dylan.

Hannah felt disappointed. She sat in a swing and Janice joined her. "Hannah, I think your idea is really neat. Maybe I could help you plan the picnic. We could work together."

That night Janice asked her father to help her print invitations. Each one gave the date and time of the picnic and suggested what food to bring. Each person was also asked to bring a small prize to be awarded at the games and races. The next day Hannah and Janice distributed the invitations to their friends. Everyone was very excited. The picnic sounded great.

The day of the picnic arrived. Hannah and Janice arranged the food on blankets and all the kids helped with the games and races. At the end of the day everyone was tired but happy. "Three cheers for Hannah and Janice," shouted Dylan. "Hip, hip, hurrah!"

It takes leaders and helpers to bring about good results. When everyone co-operates, a great deal can be accomplished.

A leader is willing to take a risk.

One night, Joey talked on the phone to his friend Elizabeth who lived in another city. She told him she was excited because tomorrow was Movie Day.

"What's that?" Joey asked.

"The last day of every month our teacher lets us watch a movie in the afternoon. It's fun!"

On the way to school the next morning, Joey wondered if maybe his teacher would do the same thing. He talked to some of the kids about it.

"But what if Ms. Barclay says no?" asked Paul.

"Or she thinks it's a terrible idea?" Colette added.

"I'll take the chance," laughed Joey.

Before setting off home for lunch, he walked up to Ms. Barclay's desk. "I was wondering if you could do what my friend's teacher does," he said.

"And what's that?" she asked.

"She lets the kids in her class watch a movie once a month."

You may not always be sure that something you want to do will succeed. It is worthwhile taking a chance and trying anyway.

Good leaders know it's important to be patient.

"That's a good idea," Ms. Barclay said. "I think a movie once a month would be a nice change."

Joey's eyes lit up. "You mean it?" he asked quickly. "We could do the same thing?"

"I'll look into it," she told him, "and see what we can arrange."

That afternoon, she told the class about Joey's idea to see what they thought. There were squeals of delight. Everyone was excited.

"The library has all sorts of interesting movies," she said. "I'll get the book that tells us about the movies we can borrow."

"I want one on volcanoes," Paul said.

"And I want to see one on airplanes and rockets!" Bobby cried.

"And could we get one about outer space?" Colette asked.

"And dinosaurs," Ryan added.

"I'm sure there are movies on all those topics," Ms. Barclay answered. "We'll find out soon enough."

The next day, the children rushed into class expecting a movie.

"Hey, where's all the movie stuff?" Paul asked.

Ms. Barclay noticed how disappointed they looked. "I'm sorry," she said. "I should have warned you that it takes time to set these things up."

Joey asked, "How long will we have to wait?"

"I don't know," she answered. "First we have to see what films there are. Then we have to arrange to get a projector."

Not long after that, the grade one class had a very pleasant surprise. At the back of the classroom was a movie projector, with a film set up. The screen had been pulled down over the blackboard.

"What movie is it?" the children asked.

"It's one that Joey suggested. This movie will show you how cartoons are made," their teacher told them as she turned out the lights and switched on the projector.

New arrangements take time. It's important not to give up or get angry when things don't happen as fast as you would like.

Leaders are people who can think for themselves. They don't wait for other people to do things first. When they see that something needs changing, they go ahead and do it. They try not to be bossy because they know it's important for everybody to have a say in a group. These are a few ways to be a good leader:

- Be willing to take the first step toward finding a solution to a problem.
- Don't give up when you run into difficulties.
- Work with others.
- Have a sense of humor.
- Expect things to come of your efforts.

Printed and bound in U.S.A.